THIS BOOK

BELONGS TO:

GW01326396

## Artful Camel Notebooks

Would you like a
FREE
download gift?
Then email us at:
happyboy@artfulcamelbooks.com
Title your email 'Happy Me'

First Published in 2020

Text and illustrations copyright © Artful Camel Books 2020

All rights reserved

ISBN-13: 979-8-6439-8801-4

artfulcamelbooks.com

# You are Special!

As you fill in this gratitude journal, with your thoughts and feelings, you will start to realise just how amazing you really are.

Keeping a journal is a great way to help you feel good, to inspire you to achieve things you wish to do, or to give you ideas for things to create.

Your journal is like a special friend, one you can share anything with, a friend who will encourage and support you, who will help you see the answers to problems.

This is your journal, you don't have to fill it in to impress others. You can't make any mistakes, anything is fine - even misspellings, smudged writing and crossing outs. It is good to write in your journal each day, so see if you can make this a regular habit, maybe each evening before you go to bed. But, if you forget to fill in a day, or don't have the time, don't worry, just carry on the next day.

At the beginning of this journal, there are several pages where you can fill in details about yourself and your life. You can start here, or if you prefer fill some in first and the rest later. Then throughout the journal there are daily pages, these have different positive statements for you to read. Some of these will be words you can repeat to yourself, or you can change them slightly so they make sense to repeat - for example, you could change 'Embrace who you are' into 'I embrace who I am'. It is good to say positive things to yourself, because it helps to make you stronger, more confident and happier, it is almost magical!

Refer back to what you have written in your journal for inspiration at any time, especially if you maybe don't feel as good as you wish.

Have fun and remember you are FABULOUS!

# Reach For The Sky

# How to use this Journal

Write the date however you like,
e.g. 13.4.20 or 13th April 2020,
or Monday 13th of April 2020.

Activity page

Quote or affirmation of the day to help you be positive.

3 things that you are grateful for each day.

Write your own quote or affirmation.

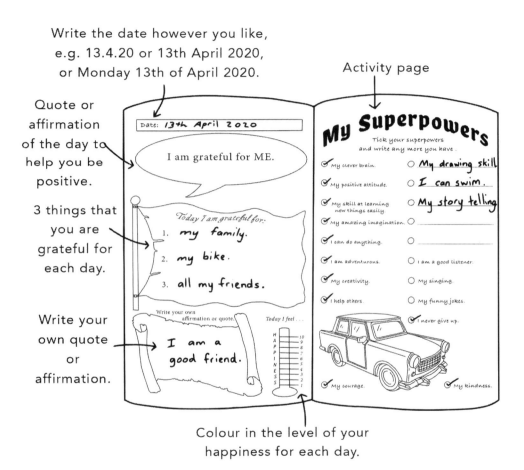

Colour in the level of your happiness for each day.

The left hand page is a daily activity to help you be more **happy**, g r a t e f u l, MINDFUL and POSITIVE.

The right hand page has thought provoking activities to i n s p i r e you.

All About ME

I Am ___ Years Old

My Name Is

I am ___ tall

MY BIRTHDAY

Draw your own unique patterns for this giraffe.

Write your birthday here.

# Self Portrait

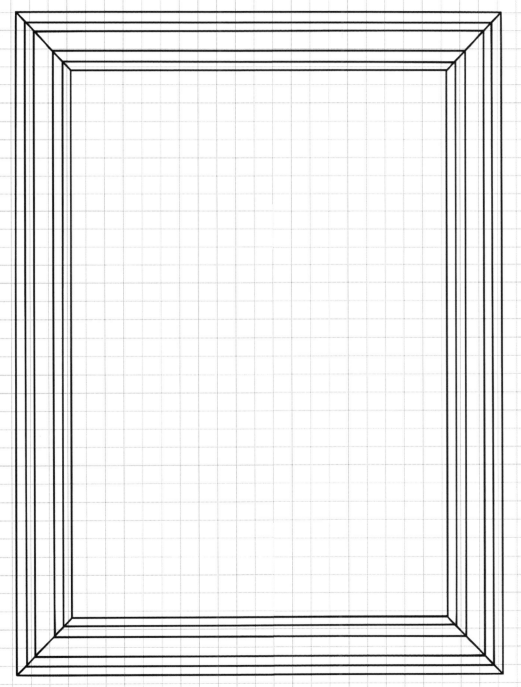

Draw or paste a picture of yourself.

When I grow up,
I want to be:

Something Interesting
About Me

# MY

# FAMILY

Draw the members of your family.

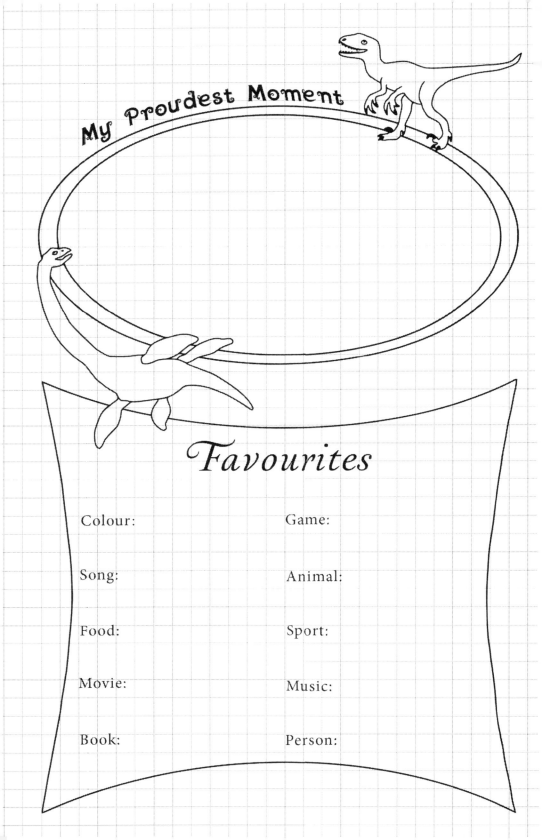

## My Proudest Moment

## Favourites

Colour:

Game:

Song:

Animal:

Food:

Sport:

Movie:

Music:

Book:

Person:

**Biggest Achievement**

**Hobbies**

Write your hobbies in the balloons.

Write your friends' names in the circles.

# Letter To Future Self

Dear Future Me,

Hello, today I am _____ years old. _____

_____

_____

_____

_____

_____

_____

_____

_____

_____

_____

_____

Love,

_____

Date:

Always keep a positive attitude.

*Today I am grateful for:*

1.

2.

3.

Write your own
affirmation or quote.

*Today I feel . . .*

H
A
P
P
I
N
E
S
S

10
9
8
7
6
5
4
3
2
1

# Positive Words About You

Write a positive word that describes
YOU on each leaf.

Date:

I am inspired to work towards my goals.

*Today I am grateful for:*

1.

2.

3.

Write your own
affirmation or quote.

*Today I feel . . .*

H
A
P
P
I
N
E
S
S

— 10
— 9
— 8
— 7
— 6
— 5
— 4
— 3
— 2
— 1

Date:

I always have what I need,
when I need it.

Today I am grateful for:

1.

2.

3.

Write your own
affirmation or quote.

Today I feel . . .

H
A
P
P
I
N
E
S
S

10
9
8
7
6
5
4
3
2
1

Date:

I wake each day rested
and full of energy.

Today I am grateful for:

1.

2.

3.

Write your own
affirmation or quote.

Today I feel . . .

H
A
P
P
I
N
E
S
S

10
9
8
7
6
5
4
3
2
1

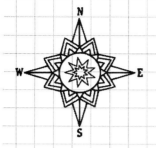

# My Inspirations

Write, draw or doodle whatever inspires you.

Date:

Surround yourself with happy and inspirational people, they will bring out the best in you.

Today I am grateful for:

1.

2.

3.

Write your own affirmation or quote.

Today I feel . . .

HAPPINESS

10
9
8
7
6
5
4
3
2
1

WRITE THE NAMES OF ALL THE PEOPLE YOU LOVE
IN THE SUN RAYS AND COLOUR THEM IN.

Date:

I am calm and contented.

*Today I am grateful for:*

1.

2.

3.

Write your own
affirmation or quote.

*Today I feel . . .*

H
A
P
P
I
N
E
S
S

10
9
8
7
6
5
4
3
2
1

# Keep CALM and colour in

Colouring in is a great
way to help yourself
relax and very often it
can calm your mind.

As you colour in this
pirate, notice: your
breathing, your
thoughts, the sound of
the pencil or pen as you
colour in.

Let yourself become
absorbed by the
colouring you are doing
and enjoy!

Date:

Courage isn't about knowing
the path to take.
It is about taking the first step.

*Today I am grateful for:*

1.

2.

3.

Write your own
affirmation or quote.

*Today I feel . . .*

H
A
P
P
I
N
E
S
S

10
9
8
7
6
5
4
3
2
1

# My Thoughts For The Week

Draw or write three things you would like to remember:

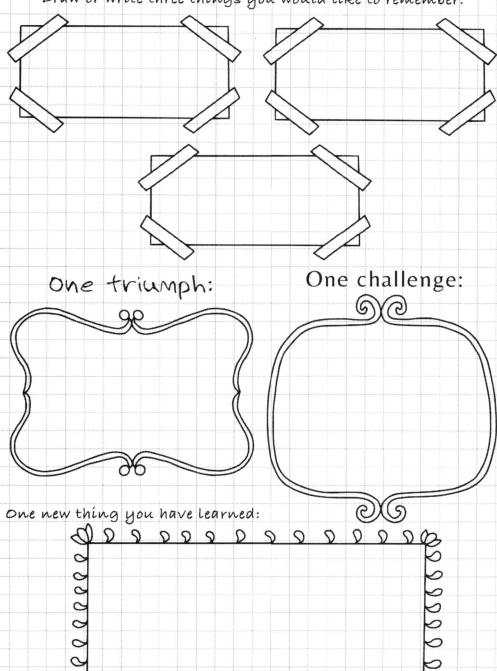

One triumph:

One challenge:

One new thing you have learned:

Date:

Be grateful for being you.
You are perfect and worthy.

*Today I am grateful for:*

1.

2.

3.

Write your own
affirmation or quote.

*Today I feel . . .*

H
A
P
P
I
N
E
S
S

10
9
8
7
6
5
4
3
2
1

# Grateful to be ME

Write or draw 3 things about yourself that you are grateful for.

Write or draw the people that you are grateful to have in your life.

What talents do you have that you are grateful for?

Date:

Your instincts are real.
TRUST YOURSELF.

Today I am grateful for:

1.

2.

3.

Write your own
affirmation or quote.

Today I feel . . .

HAPPINESS

10
9
8
7
6
5
4
3
2
1

**Date:**

I choose to always be kind
to myself and others.

*Today I am grateful for:*

1.

2.

3.

Write your own
affirmation or quote.

*Today I feel . . .*

HAPPINESS

10
9
8
7
6
5
4
3
2
1

Date:

I spread joy everywhere I go.

*Today I am grateful for:*

1.

2.

3.

Write your own
affirmation or quote.

*Today I feel . . .*

H
A
P
P
I
N
E
S
S

10
9
8
7
6
5
4
3
2
1

# Spread The Joy With A Happy Stone . . .

Decorating a stone or rock with a positive picture or word and giving it to someone is a great way to cheer them up or put a smile on their face.

## You will need:

*A flat stone or rock
*Permanent markers
*Acrylic paint and brushes
*Old newspaper
*Top coat varnish

Remember to ask an adult for permission, before you start this activity.

1. You can get stones or rocks from the garden, on the beach or buy them from the shop.

2. Wash your stone to clean off dirt, mud or sand.

3. Let the stone dry completely.

4. Lay out old newspaper on your work top.

5. Paint or draw your stone with a positive picture, e.g. a smiley face or a positive word, e.g. love.

6. Leave the stone to dry before you paint or spray with the top coat varnish, to protect the stone from water.

Draw the picture or word of your stone here, before giving it away.

Give the finished stone to a friend, someone you love or someone who you think might need cheering up. You can also leave it around for someone to find.

have fun ♡

Date:

I am a winner.

Today I am grateful for:

1.

2.

3.

Write your own
affirmation or quote.

Today I feel . . .

H
A
P
P
I
N
E
S
S

10
9
8
7
6
5
4
3
2
1

Date:

I am smart
and make good choices.

Today I am grateful for:

1.

2.

3.

Write your own
affirmation or quote.

Today I feel . . .

H
A
P
P
I
N
E
S
S

10
9
8
7
6
5
4
3
2
1

Date:

Positive thinking makes my life better and also makes life better for those around me.

*Today I am grateful for:*

1.

2.

3.

Write your own affirmation or quote.

*Today I feel . . .*

H
A
P
P
I
N
E
S
S

10
9
8
7
6
5
4
3
2
1

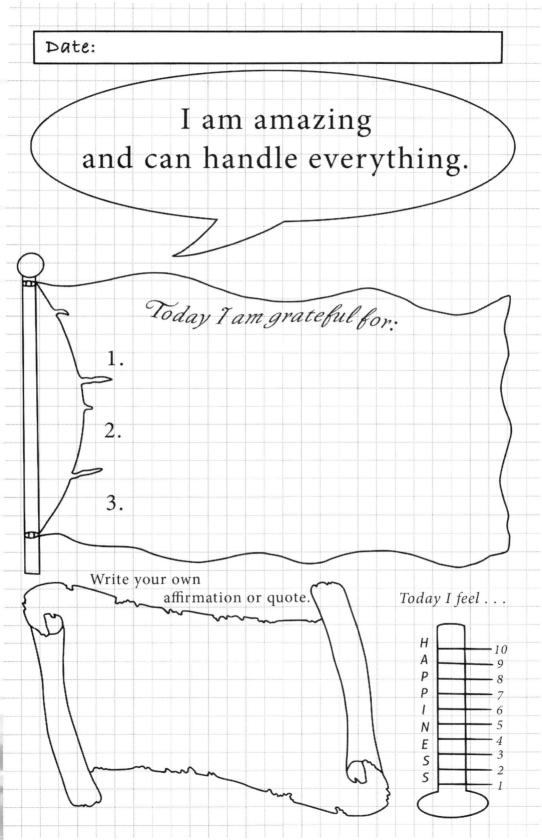

Date:

I am amazing
and can handle everything.

Today I am grateful for:

1.

2.

3.

Write your own
affirmation or quote.

Today I feel . . .

HAPPINESS

10
9
8
7
6
5
4
3
2
1

Date:

I believe in myself.

*Today I am grateful for:*

1.

2.

3.

Write your own
affirmation or quote.

*Today I feel . . .*

HAPPINESS

10
9
8
7
6
5
4
3
2
1

# SELF LOVE

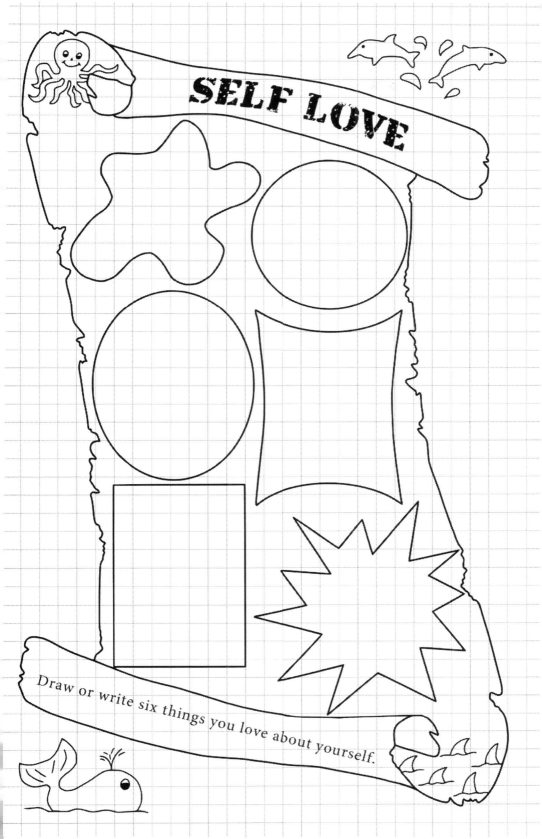

Draw or write six things you love about yourself.

Date:

You are braver than you believe,
stronger than you seem
and smarter than you think.

Today I am grateful for:

1.

2.

3.

Write your own
affirmation or quote.

Today I feel . . .

H
A
P
P
I
N
E
S
S

10
9
8
7
6
5
4
3
2
1

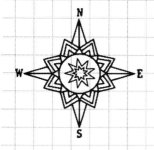

# My Inspirations

Write, draw or doodle whatever inspires you.

Date:

I achieve whatever
I set out to do.

Today I am grateful for:

1.

2.

3.

Write your own
affirmation or quote.

Today I feel . . .

H
A
P
P
I
N
E
S
S

10
9
8
7
6
5
4
3
2
1

# My Superpowers

Tick your superpowers
and write any more you have .

○ My clever brain.               ○ _____

○ My positive attitude.          ○ _____

○ My skill at learning           ○ _____
   new things easily.

○ My amazing imagination.        ○ _____

○ I can do anything.             ○ _____

○ I am adventurous.              ○ I am a good listener.

○ My creativity.                 ○ My singing.

○ I help others.                 ○ My funny jokes.

                                 ○ I never give up.

○ My courage.                    ○ My kindness.

**Date:**

The best things in life are free:
hugs, smiles, kisses, friends, family, love,
sleep, laughter and good memories.

*Today I am grateful for:*

1.

2.

3.

Write your own
affirmation or quote.

*Today I feel . . .*

HAPPINESS

10
9
8
7
6
5
4
3
2
1

Date:

I replace every negative thought with a positive thought.

Today I am grateful for:

1.

2.

3.

Write your own affirmation or quote.

Today I feel . . .

H
A
P
P
I
N
E
S
S

10
9
8
7
6
5
4
3
2
1

**Date:**

Don't be afraid to make mistakes. Learn from them and then move on as a wiser person.

*Today I am grateful for:*

1.

2.

3.

Write your own affirmation or quote.

*Today I feel . . .*

HAPPINESS

10
9
8
7
6
5
4
3
2
1

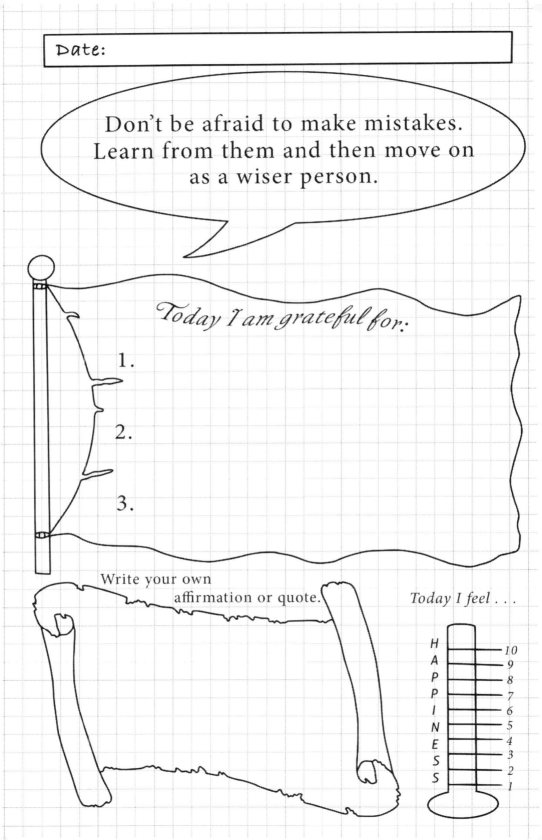

# My Thoughts For The Week

Draw or write three things you would like to remember:

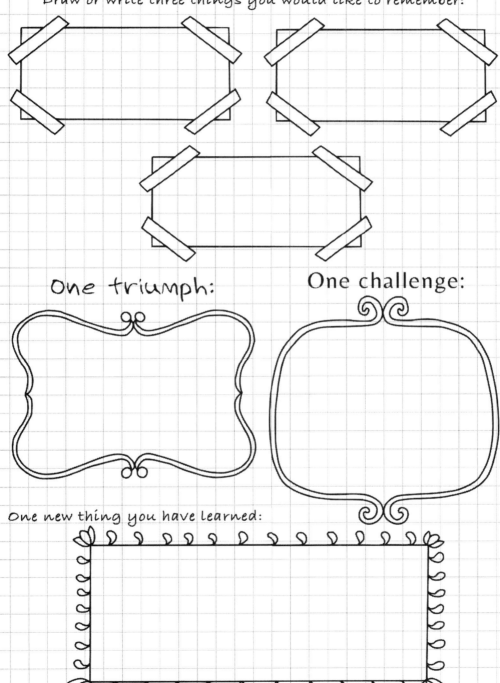

One triumph:

One challenge:

One new thing you have learned:

**Date:**

SMILE
because you are wonderful,
because you are amazing,
because you are unique
and because you can.

*Today I am grateful for:*

1.

2.

3.

Write your own
affirmation or quote.

*Today I feel . . .*

HAPPINESS

10
9
8
7
6
5
4
3
2
1

# What makes YOU happy?

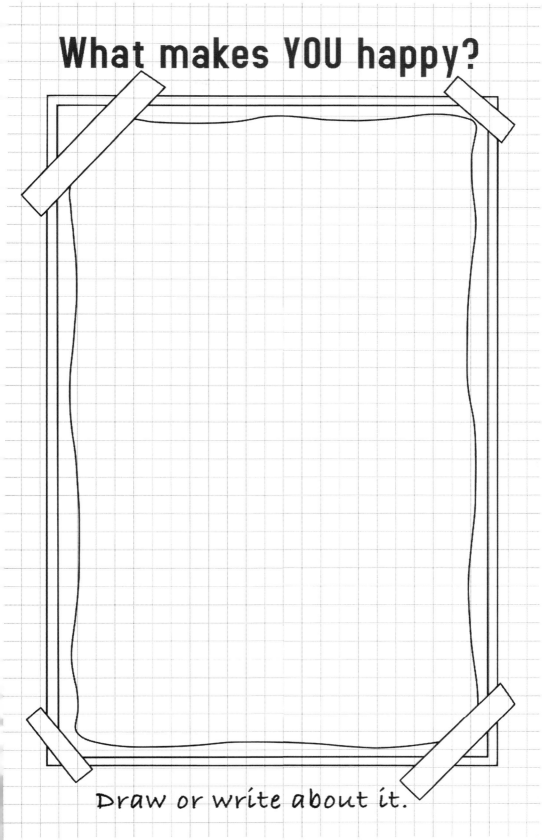

Draw or write about it.

Date:

I treat my body with love and respect.

*Today I am grateful for:*

1.

2.

3.

Write your own affirmation or quote.

*Today I feel . . .*

HAPPINESS

10
9
8
7
6
5
4
3
2
1

**Date:**

I am clever, because that is what I choose to be.

*Today I am grateful for:*

1.

2.

3.

Write your own affirmation or quote.

*Today I feel . . .*

HAPPINESS

10
9
8
7
6
5
4
3
2
1

Date:

Always believe that something wonderful is about to happen.

*Today I am grateful for:*

1.

2.

3.

Write your own
affirmation or quote.

*Today I feel . . .*

H
A
P
P
I
N
E
S
S

10
9
8
7
6
5
4
3
2
1

Draw or write something

# awesome

that happened today.

Date:

I accept myself for who I am.

Today I am grateful for:

1.

2.

3.

Write your own
affirmation or quote.

Today I feel . . .

H
A
P
P
I
N
E
S
S

10
9
8
7
6
5
4
3
2
1

# What does it mean to *YOU* to be yourself?

Date:

I am a magnet for joy,
love and abundance.

Today I am grateful for:

1.

2.

3.

Write your own
affirmation or quote.

Today I feel . . .

HAPPINESS

10
9
8
7
6
5
4
3
2
1

Date:

Embrace who you are.

Today I am grateful for:

1.

2.

3.

Write your own
affirmation or quote.

Today I feel . . .

H
A
P
P
I
N
E
S
S

10
9
8
7
6
5
4
3
2
1

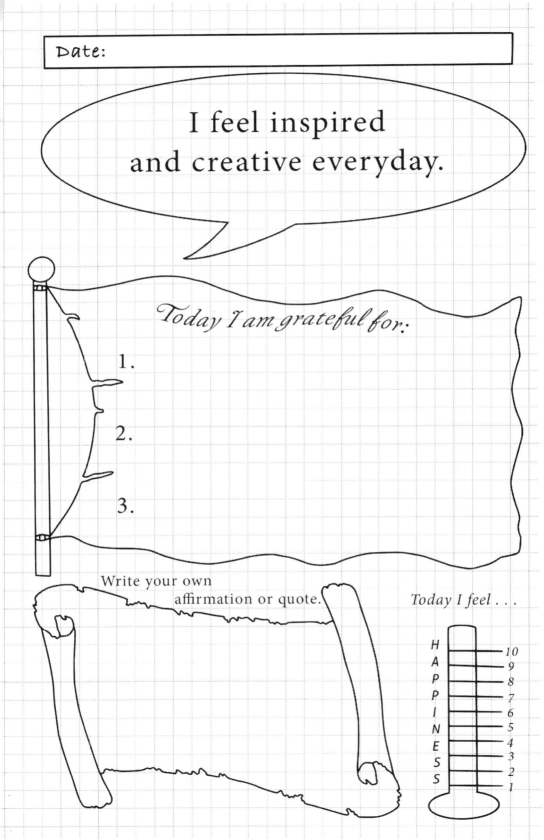

Date:

I feel inspired
and creative everyday.

Today I am grateful for:

1.

2.

3.

Write your own
affirmation or quote.

Today I feel . . .

H
A
P
P
I
N
E
S
S

10
9
8
7
6
5
4
3
2
1

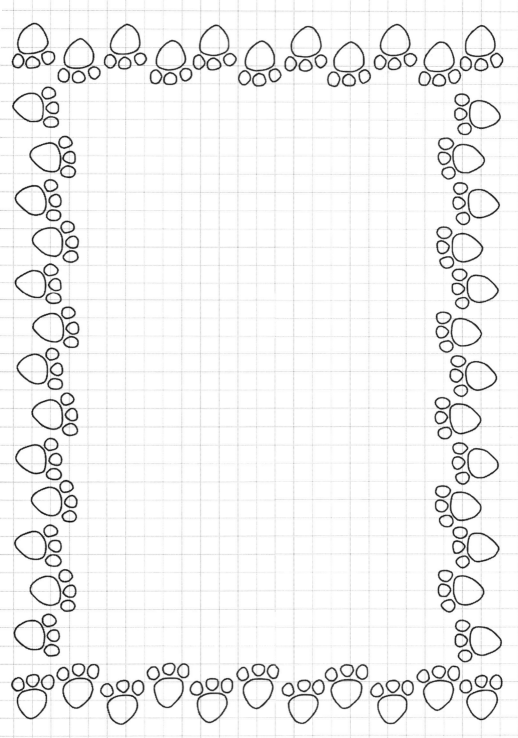

If you were an animal, what animal
would you like to be and why?

Date:

You were born to shine.

*Today I am grateful for:*

1.

2.

3.

Write your own
affirmation or quote.

*Today I feel . . .*

HAPPINESS

10
9
8
7
6
5
4
3
2
1

Date:

I take great care
of my body and mind.

Today I am grateful for:

1.

2.

3.

Write your own
affirmation or quote.

Today I feel . . .

H
A
P
P
I
N
E
S
S

10
9
8
7
6
5
4
3
2
1

Date:

I AM
two very powerful words,
for what you put after
them you become.

Today I am grateful for:

1.

2.

3.

Write your own
affirmation or quote.

Today I feel . . .

H
A
P
P
I
N
E
S
S

10
9
8
7
6
5
4
3
2
1

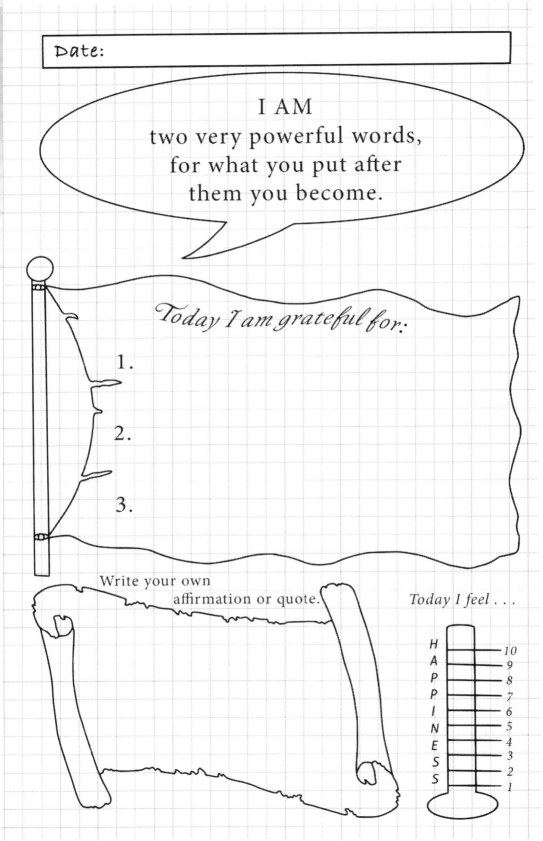

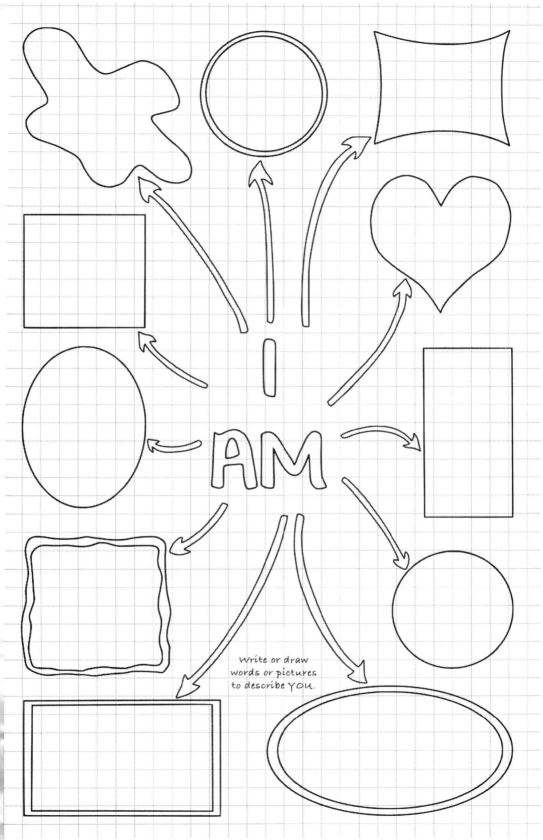

I AM

Write or draw words or pictures to describe YOU.

Date:

How you see yourself
is how you create yourself.

*Today I am grateful for:*

1.

2.

3.

Write your own
affirmation or quote.

*Today I feel . . .*

H
A
P
P
I
N
E
S
S

10
9
8
7
6
5
4
3
2
1

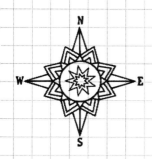

# My Inspirations

Write, draw or doodle whatever inspires you.

Date:

It is cool to be kind.

*Today I am grateful for:*

1.

2.

3.

Write your own
affirmation or quote.

*Today I feel . . .*

HAPPINESS

10
9
8
7
6
5
4
3
2
1

# Kindness

Kind things I have done for people.

Kind things people have done for me.

Date:

What you think, you become.
What you feel, you attract.
What you imagine, you create.

Today I am grateful for:

1.

2.

3.

Write your own
affirmation or quote.

Today I feel . . .

HAPPINESS

10
9
8
7
6
5
4
3
2
1

# My Thoughts For The Week

Draw or write three things you would like to remember:

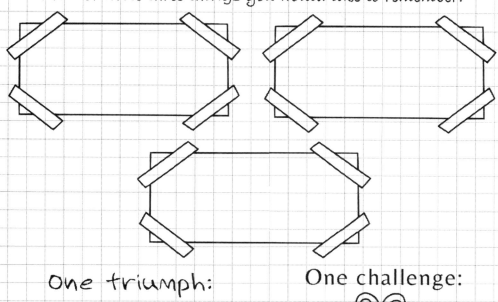

## One triumph:

## One challenge:

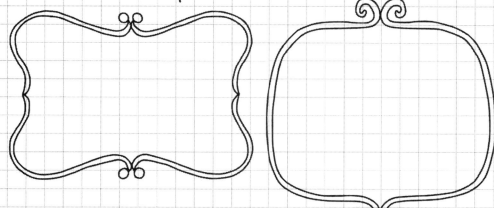

One new thing you have learned:

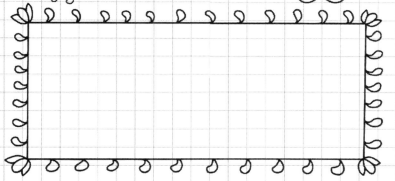

**Date:**

Every day brings me
opportunities and
possibilities.

*Today I am grateful for:*

1.

2.

3.

Write your own
affirmation or quote.

*Today I feel . . .*

H
A
P
P
I
N
E
S
S

10
9
8
7
6
5
4
3
2
1

# HAIR STYLE

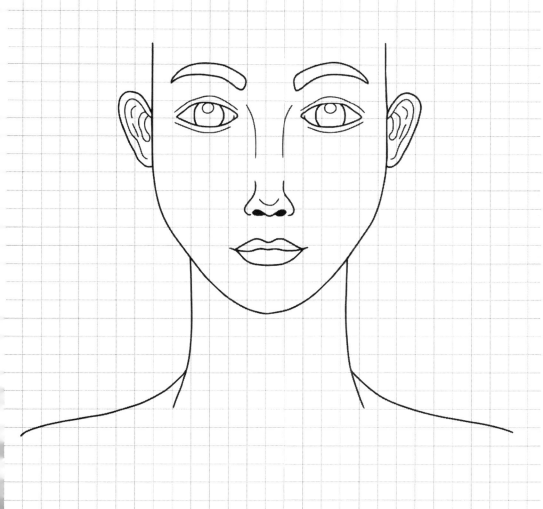

Draw the hair style that you think would be FUN to have.

Date:

Be your own sun.
Be your own moon.
You don't need anyone else
to help you shine.

*Today I am grateful for:*

1.

2.

3.

Write your own
affirmation or quote.

*Today I feel . . .*

H
A
P
P
I
N
E
S
S

10
9
8
7
6
5
4
3
2
1

Date:

I keep an open mind.

Today I am grateful for:

1.

2.

3.

Write your own
affirmation or quote.

Today I feel . . .

H
A
P
P
I
N
E
S
S

10
9
8
7
6
5
4
3
2
1

Date:

Every day I am growing
and learning.

Today I am grateful for:

1.

2.

3.

Write your own
affirmation or quote.

Today I feel . . .

H
A
P
P
I
N
E
S
S

10
9
8
7
6
5
4
3
2
1

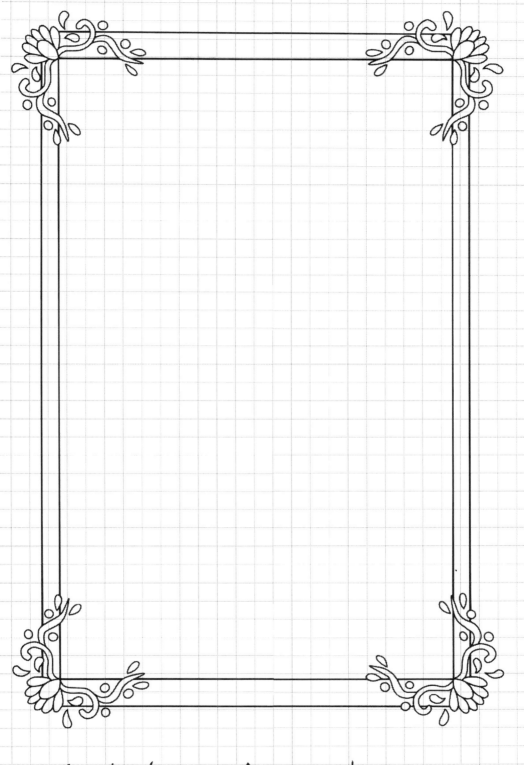

A picture drawn by me.

Date:

I nurture my friendships.

Today I am grateful for:

1.

2.

3.

Write your own
affirmation or quote.

Today I feel . . .

H
A
P
P
I
N
E
S
S

10
9
8
7
6
5
4
3
2
1

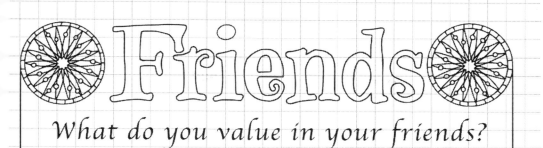

# Friends

## What do you value in your friends?

Draw or write them here.

Friends

**Date:**

Everything is possible.

*Today I am grateful for:*

1.

2.

3.

Write your own
affirmation or quote.

*Today I feel . . .*

H
A
P
P
I
N
E
S
S

10
9
8
7
6
5
4
3
2
1

Date:

My life is full of so many things to be grateful for.

Today I am grateful for:

1.

2.

3.

Write your own affirmation or quote.

Today I feel . . .

H
A
P
P
I
N
E
S
S

10
9
8
7
6
5
4
3
2
1

Date:

YOU ARE UNIQUE

Today I am grateful for:

1.

2.

3.

Write your own
affirmation or quote.

Today I feel . . .

HAPPINESS

10
9
8
7
6
5
4
3
2
1

# WE ARE ALL STARS
## BUT EACH OF US IS UNIQUE

Draw your unique star in the space above.

Date:

I believe in my abilities
to learn new skills.

Today I am grateful for:

1.

2.

3.

Write your own
affirmation or quote.

Today I feel . . .

HAPPINESS

10
9
8
7
6
5
4
3
2
1

# I would like to learn how to

Write and draw a picture.

Date:

HAPPINESS
is not about getting what you want,
it is about appreciating
what you have.

*Today I am grateful for:*

1.

2.

3.

Write your own
affirmation or quote.

*Today I feel . . .*

HAPPINESS
10
9
8
7
6
5
4
3
2
1

Say out loud, or in your head, HAPPY AFFIRMATIONS
about YOURSELF as you colour in this picture.

Date:

I am grateful for ME.

*Today I am grateful for:*

1.

2.

3.

Write your own
affirmation or quote.

*Today I feel . . .*

H
A
P
P
I
N
E
S
S

10
9
8
7
6
5
4
3
2
1

Date:

Every day is a different day, with different experiences.

*Today I am grateful for:*

1.

2.

3.

Write your own affirmation or quote.

*Today I feel . . .*

H
A
P
P
I
N
E
S
S

10
9
8
7
6
5
4
3
2
1

**Date:**

> Start and end your day with gratitude.

*Today I am grateful for:*

1.

2.

3.

Write your own affirmation or quote.

*Today I feel . . .*

HAPPINESS

10
9
8
7
6
5
4
3
2
1

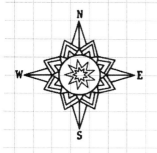

# My Inspirations

Write, draw or doodle whatever inspires you.

Date:

I act with courage
and confidence.

Today I am grateful for:

1.

2.

3.

Write your own
affirmation or quote.

Today I feel . . .

H
A
P
P
I
N
E
S
S

10
9
8
7
6
5
4
3
2
1

# My Superpowers

Choose one of your many SUPERPOWERS
and design a costume for this superpower.

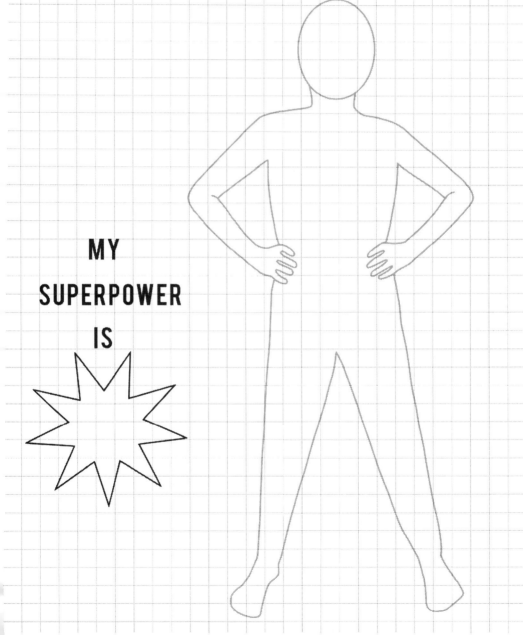

MY

SUPERPOWER

IS

Date:

I am loved.

Today I am grateful for:

1.

2.

3.

Write your own
affirmation or quote.

Today I feel . . .

H
A
P
P
I
N
E
S
S

10
9
8
7
6
5
4
3
2
1

# One Thing...

That makes you smile.

That you love to talk about.

That you wear all the time.

That you ate that was so delicious.

To do for fun.

Date:

I take the time to show my friends that I care about them.

Today I am grateful for:

1.

2.

3.

Write your own affirmation or quote.

Today I feel . . .

H
A
P
P
I
N
E
S
S

10
9
8
7
6
5
4
3
2
1

# CELEBRATING FRIENDSHIP

My friend's name is:

How and when we met:

A picture of my friend:

Things we do together:

Three words to describe my friend:

Date:

I believe in my dreams.

*Today I am grateful for:*

1.

2.

3.

Write your own affirmation or quote.

*Today I feel . . .*

H
A
P
P
I
N
E
S
S

10
9
8
7
6
5
4
3
2
1

If you could have one wish, what would it be and why?

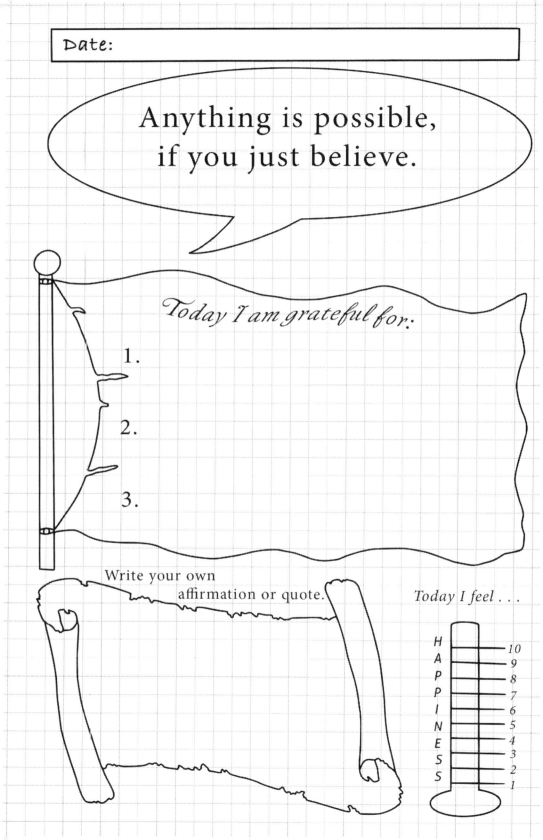

Date:

Anything is possible,
if you just believe.

Today I am grateful for:

1.

2.

3.

Write your own
affirmation or quote.

Today I feel . . .

HAPPINESS
10
9
8
7
6
5
4
3
2
1

Date:

It is alright to make mistakes.

Today I am grateful for:

1.

2.

3.

Write your own
affirmation or quote.

Today I feel . . .

HAPPINESS

10
9
8
7
6
5
4
3
2
1

Date:

I am successful in whatever I choose to do.

Today I am grateful for:

1.

2.

3.

Write your own affirmation or quote.

Today I feel . . .

HAPPINESS

10
9
8
7
6
5
4
3
2
1

Who is the coolest person you know,
in real life, a celebrity or anybody?

What makes them so fantastic and why?

What do you have in common with them?

Date:

Everything is always working out for me.

Today I am grateful for:

1.

2.

3.

Write your own affirmation or quote.

Today I feel . . .

H
A
P
P
I
N
E
S
S

10
9
8
7
6
5
4
3
2
1

# My Thoughts For The Week

Draw or write three things you would like to remember:

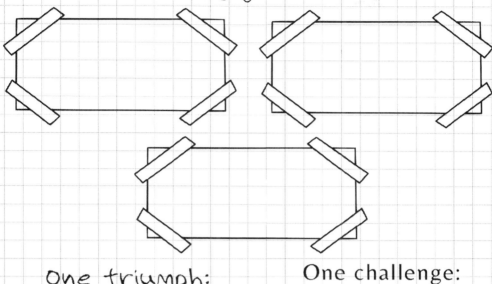

One triumph:

One challenge:

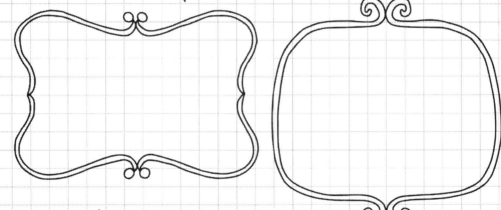

One new thing you have learned:

Date:

I am healthy
and full of energy.

*Today I am grateful for:*

1.

2.

3.

Write your own
affirmation or quote.

*Today I feel . . .*

HAPPINESS
10
9
8
7
6
5
4
3
2
1

# Things I Am Good At
## And Do Well

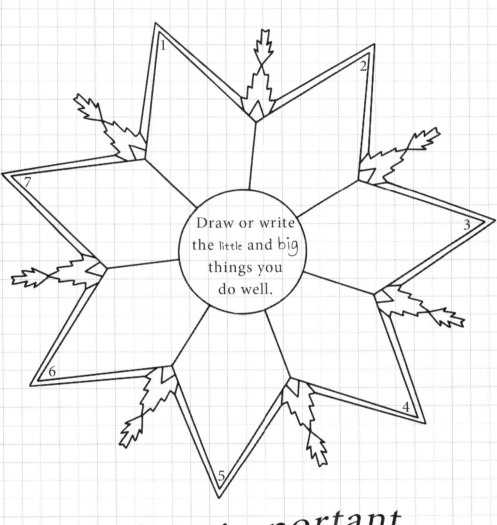

Draw or write the little and big things you do well.

*It is important to celebrate all your* **achievements.**

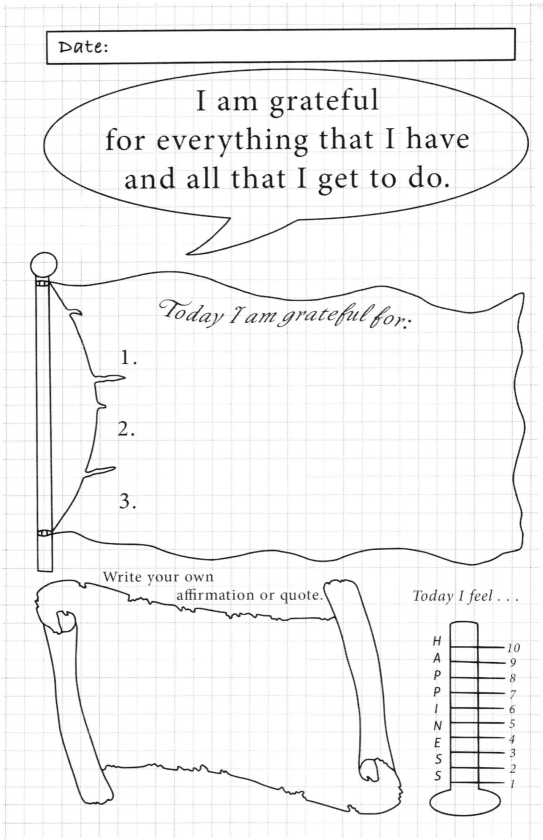

**Date:**

> I am grateful for everything that I have and all that I get to do.

*Today I am grateful for:*

1.

2.

3.

Write your own affirmation or quote.

*Today I feel . . .*

HAPPINESS

10
9
8
7
6
5
4
3
2
1

# Thank You
## *Letter*

*Dear* _____

# Thank You

*for* _____

_____

_____

_____

_____

_____

_____

_____

_____

_____

_____

_____

*Love from* _____

*To show your appreciation, write a*
*'Thank You' letter to someone who has*
*recently done something kind for you.*

Date:

Life is better when you laugh.
So, fill your day with laughter!

*Today I am grateful for:*

1.

2.

3.

Write your own
affirmation or quote.

*Today I feel . . .*

H
A
P
P
I
N
E
S
S

10
9
8
7
6
5
4
3
2
1

What was the **funniest** thing that happened today or this week that made you **laugh?**

*hee! hee!*

*ho! ho!*

*ha! ha!*

Draw or write about it.

*hee! hee!*

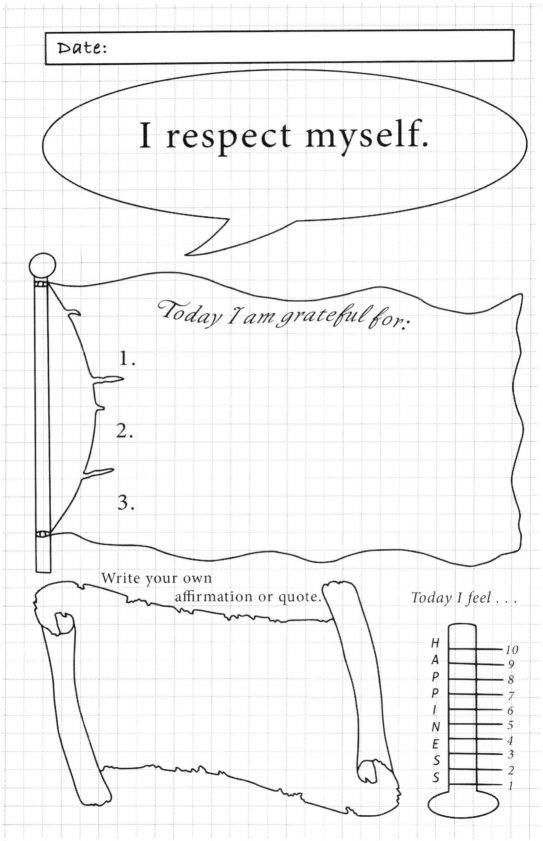

Date:

I respect myself.

Today I am grateful for:

1.

2.

3.

Write your own
affirmation or quote.

Today I feel . . .

HAPPINESS

10
9
8
7
6
5
4
3
2
1

# This is me

Draw a <u>detailed</u> picture of yourself
and label interesting features of your body.

Date:

I can make a difference
in this world.

Today I am grateful for:

1.

2.

3.

Write your own
affirmation or quote.

Today I feel . . .

H
A
P
P
I
N
E
S
S

10
9
8
7
6
5
4
3
2
1

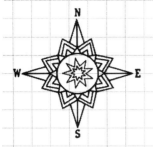

# My Inspirations

Write, draw or doodle whatever inspires you.

Date:

I have many talents.

Today I am grateful for:

1.

2.

3.

Write your own
affirmation or quote.

Today I feel . . .

HAPPINESS

10
9
8
7
6
5
4
3
2
1

# MY T-SHIRT DESIGN

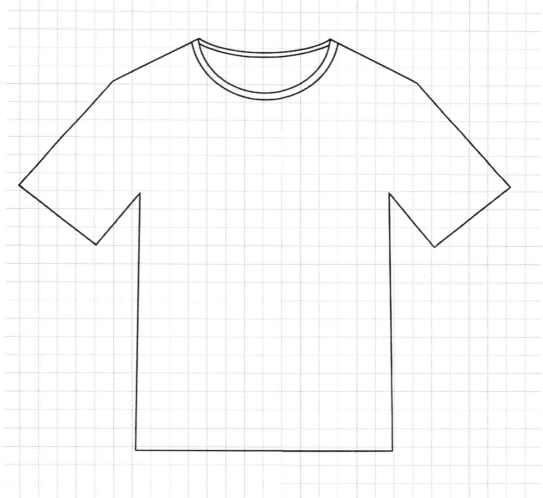

Design your own T-shirt.

Date:

I am courageous.

Today I am grateful for:

1.

2.

3.

Write your own
affirmation or quote.

Today I feel . . .

H
A
P
P
I
N
E
S
S

10
9
8
7
6
5
4
3
2
1

# Treasure Chest

If you buried a treasure chest for the future,
what would you put in it and why?

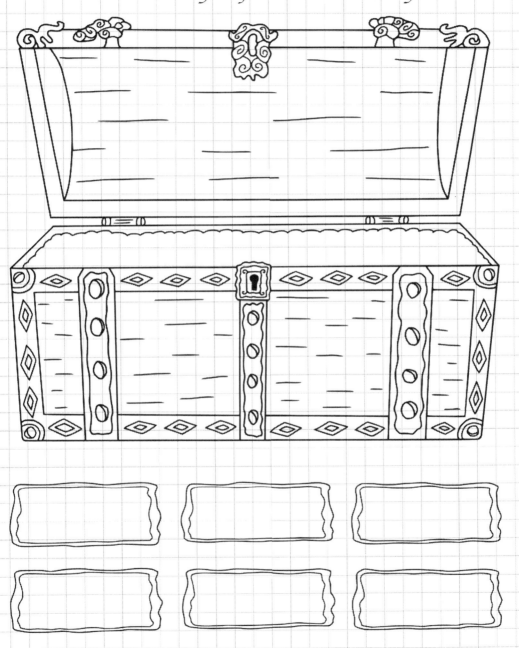

Draw them in the treasure chest and write them in the boxes.

Date:

I enjoy learning new things.

Today I am grateful for:

1.

2.

3.

Write your own
affirmation or quote.

Today I feel . . .

HAPPINESS

10
9
8
7
6
5
4
3
2
1

Date:

Believe you can
and you are halfway there.

Today I am grateful for:

1.

2.

3.

Write your own
affirmation or quote.

Today I feel . . .

H
A
P
P
I
N
E
S
S

10
9
8
7
6
5
4
3
2
1

Date:

I am safe and protected.

Today I am grateful for:

1.

2.

3.

Write your own
affirmation or quote.

Today I feel . . .

H
A
P
P
I
N
E
S
S

10
9
8
7
6
5
4
3
2
1

# Keep CALM and colour in

Colouring in is a great way to help yourself relax and very often it can calm your mind.

As you colour in this dinosaur, notice: your breathing, your thoughts, the sound of the pencil or pen as you colour in.

Let yourself become absorbed by the colouring you are doing and enjoy!

Date:

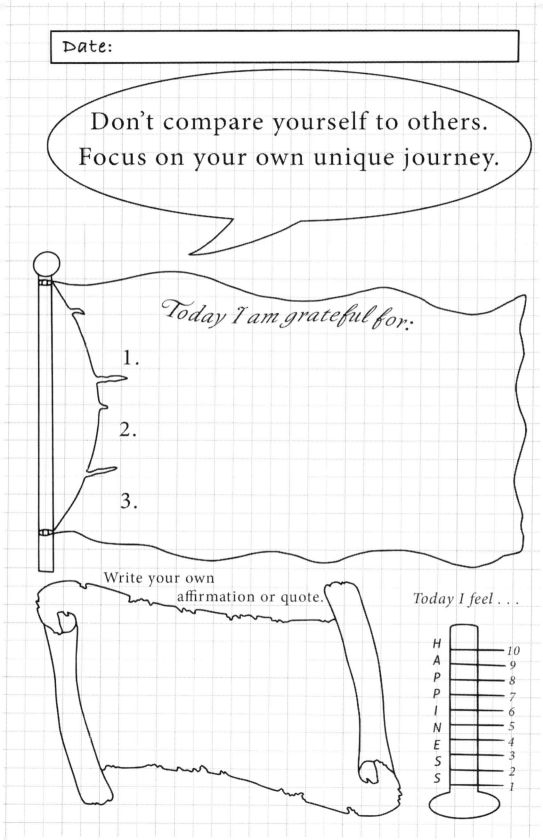

Don't compare yourself to others.
Focus on your own unique journey.

Today I am grateful for:

1.

2.

3.

Write your own
affirmation or quote.

Today I feel . . .

H
A
P
P
I
N
E
S
S

10
9
8
7
6
5
4
3
2
1

Date:

I am a good listener.

Today I am grateful for:

1.

2.

3.

Write your own
affirmation or quote.

Today I feel . . .

HAPPINESS

10
9
8
7
6
5
4
3
2
1

Date:

Choose to see goodness
and beauty in the world.

*Today I am grateful for:*

1.

2.

3.

Write your own
affirmation or quote.

*Today I feel . . .*

H
A
P
P
I
N
E
S
S

10
9
8
7
6
5
4
3
2
1

## Life Is Beautiful

When you are outside, observe your surroundings. Notice the
sounds, the people, the animals and nature.
Draw or describe what you see.

Date:

I am confident.

*Today I am grateful for:*

1.

2.

3.

Write your own
affirmation or quote.

*Today I feel . . .*

HAPPINESS

10
9
8
7
6
5
4
3
2
1

# My Thoughts For The Week

Draw or write three things you would like to remember:

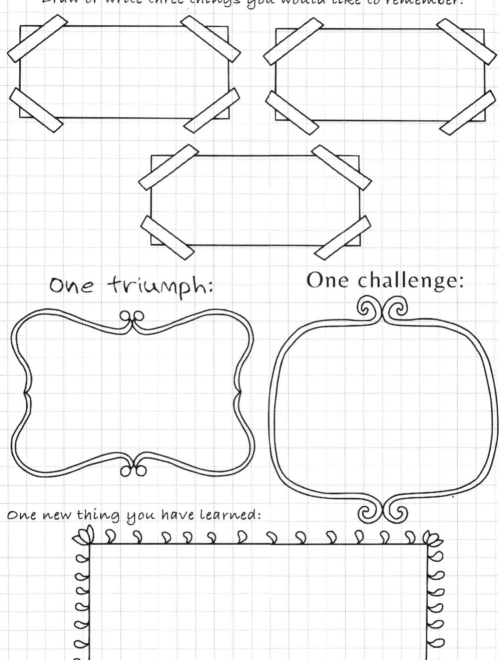

One triumph:

One challenge:

One new thing you have learned:

Date:

Wonderful things
happen to me.

Today I am grateful for:

1.

2.

3.

Write your own
affirmation or quote.

Today I feel . . .

H
A
P
P
I
N
E
S
S

10
9
8
7
6
5
4
3
2
1

If you were to create a fantasy car, plane, or spaceship, what would it look like?

Date:

I am a good friend.

Today I am grateful for:

1.

2.

3.

Write your own
affirmation or quote.

Today I feel . . .

HAPPINESS
10
9
8
7
6
5
4
3
2
1

# Celebrating Friendship

My friend's name
is:

How and when we met:

A picture of my friend:

Things we do together:

Three words to describe
my friend:

Date:

I am proud of myself.

Today I am grateful for:

1.

2.

3.

Write your own
affirmation or quote.

Today I feel . . .

HAPPINESS

10
9
8
7
6
5
4
3
2
1

Date:

I can thrive beyond
my comfort zone.

*Today I am grateful for:*

1.

2.

3.

Write your own
affirmation or quote.

*Today I feel . . .*

H
A
P
P
I
N
E
S
S

10
9
8
7
6
5
4
3
2
1

Date:

My challenges help me grow.

Today I am grateful for:

1.

2.

3.

Write your own
affirmation or quote.

Today I feel . . .

H
A
P
P
I
N
E
S
S

— 10
— 9
— 8
— 7
— 6
— 5
— 4
— 3
— 2
— 1

# Positive Wordsearch

```
A C O N F I D E N T U S
M R Z I W M O T E I G O
X E V Y P A Z U H G R S
H A P P Y G Q U N P A U
O T J L M I B I C N T O
N I O D N N Z L F R E E
E V Y U K A M U R V F G
S E F T M T S V O S U A
T W U A W I V L J M L R
B E L I E V E O N I D U
V T P O W E R F U L E O
S E D T A L E N T E D C
```

16 words relating to a positive attitude.
You can find these words: horizontally, vertically, diagonally and in any direction.

| | | | |
|---|---|---|---|
| AMAZING | BELIEVE | CONFIDENT | COURAGEOUS |
| CREATIVE | FREE | GRATEFUL | HAPPY |
| HONEST | IMAGINATIVE | JOYFUL | LOVE |
| POWERFUL | SMILE | TALENTED | UNIQUE |

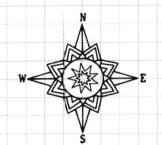

# My Inspirations

Write, draw or doodle whatever inspires you.

**Date:**

YOU CAN
end of story!

*Today I am grateful for:*

1.

2.

3.

Write your own
affirmation or quote.

*Today I feel . . .*

H
A
P
P
I
N
E
S
S

10
9
8
7
6
5
4
3
2
1

We hope you have enjoyed filling out your Happy Me Journal.

If you would like another happiness journal - a personalised copy with your name on the front cover (as in the 'Harry' example below), or one without a name - please visit our website, where we have up to date details on these and other books in our catalogue.

If you can't find your name, just send us an email and we will create one with your name.

Thank you.

artfulcamelbooks.com

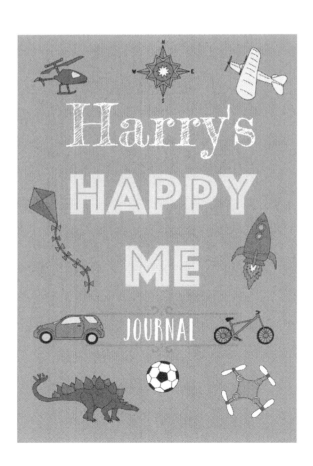

Printed in Great Britain
by Amazon

61446913R00083